GW00859016

The Precio Pearl

Matthew 13: God is Best

CATHERINE MACKENZIE
Illustrated by Chiara Bertelli

CF4•K

Learn it: God's kingdom lasts forever
Do it: Ask God to forgive you.
Find it: What does God give? John 3:16

If you knew where to find a treasure chest, what would you do? Would you spend days digging it up? Would you give lots of money to make sure the treasure became yours?

What if the treasure was the best treasure in the world? Would you spend all the money you had so that the treasure could be yours?

Jesus told two stories — one was about a man who discovered some amazin treasure.

Jesus said, 'The kingdom of heaven is like a treasure hidden in a field which a man found and hid again.' He was so glad to find the treasure tha he immediately went and sold all that he had, so he could buy the field fo himself and make the treasure his.

Jesus also told a story about a man who discovered a precious stone calle[d] a pearl. Jesus said, 'The kingdom of heaven is like a merchant seeking fin[e] pearls.' When the merchant found one very precious pearl of great value[,] he immediately went and sold all that he had so that he could buy that pear[l] for himself.

What does Jesus want you to learn from these two stories?

He wants you to realise that God's forgiveness is very precious. Treasure is valuable. Jewels are valuable.

A security guard watches over the expensive rings and necklaces, but salvation is even more valuable than gold and silver.

WHAT IS SALVATION? All people disobey God and are sinners. You need to be forgiven for the wrong things you do. If you aren't forgiven then you won't be with God. There will be no love or joy or peace. That is what hell is. However, God wants to save sinners. God wants to change you so that you love and trust in him. He wants to bring you into his family and give you everlasting life.

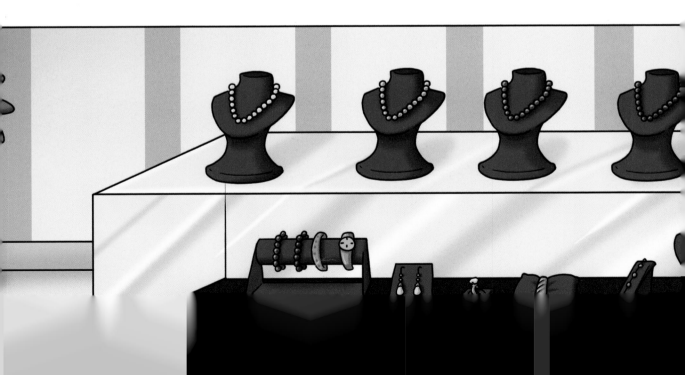

Salvation is more valuable than jewels. Jewels don't last forever and they can be destroyed or stolen. Salvation cannot be destroyed. Once you have salvation it is never taken away.

Very few people find treasure. If they do they are often surprised! They shout out, 'Look what I've found!' When you realise how kind and loving God is, you too will gasp in amazement. 'God is so good! He is willing to take away my sin. I don't deserve it but he still wants to save me. Isn't he amazing?'

Another thing that Jesus wants you to realise is that salvation is costly. The man who found the pearl sold everything that he had so he could buy it.

He didn't mind the cost because he knew that the precious stone was a real treasure.

Salvation is better than the costliest treasure. When you are saved, you become part of God's family. God is truly valuable. There is nothing and no one better than him. He is always good, no matter what is happening in our lives.

You don't have to pay money to be saved by God — but God had to give his Son so that sinners could be saved.

Jesus, God's Son, had to give his life. He had to be punished instead of sinners. That is a great cost.

But, just because salvation is free doesn't mean you do nothing. God ha
good works for you to do. These good works are love, joy, peace, patience
kindness, goodness, faithfulness, gentleness, self-control. When you do
things like this you show other people what God is like. However, these
good works can never pay God back for what he has done.

Jewels, and treasure, clothes and houses, money and fame — all of these things only last for a short time. Many things that we buy are soon thrown out. But God's love is forever, his kingdom is forever. Salvation is for ever. That's far more valuable. It is the most valuable!

You definitely should want to find the best treasure ever! Well, that bes
treasure is God. Ask God to forgive you for the wrong things you have done
Ask him to help you trust in him and obey him. Show people how lovely God
is by doing things that please God.

You would be glad if a friend found some wonderful treasure. When you
find God's eternal treasure you will want your friends to find him too!

The man with the treasure field was thrilled. The merchant who bought the pearl was delighted. Once they had made their precious discoveries, they did everything they could to make sure the treasure was theirs.

Being in God's family is the best treasure ever. Make sure that this treasure is yours.

Turn away from sin. Trust in God. Believe in Jesus.

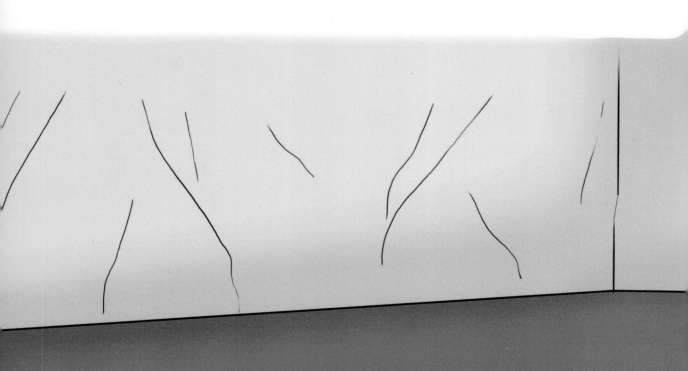

Christian Focus Publications

Christian Focus Publications publishes books for adults and children under its four main imprints: Christian Focus, CF4K, Mentor and Christian Heritage. Our books reflect our conviction that God's Word is reliable and Jesus is the way to know him, and live for ever with him. Our children's list includes a Sunday School curriculum that covers pre-school to early teens, and puzzle and activity books. We also publish personal and family devotional titles, biographies and inspirational stories that children will love. If you are looking for quality Bible teaching for children then we have an excellent range of Bible stories and age-specific theological books. From pre-school board books to teenage apologetics, we have it covered!

AUTHOR'S DEDICATON: To my friends and family at Kingsview Christian Centre, A.P.C.

10 9 8 7 6 5 4 3 2 1

Copyright © 2017 Catherine Mackenzie

ISBN: 978-1-5271-0096-1

Published in 2017 by Christian Focus Publications Ltd.

Geanies House, Fearn, Tain, Ross-shire, IV20 1TW, Great Britain

Illustrations by Chiara Bertelli

Cover Design: Sarah Korvemaker

Printed in Malta